This boo

If found, please contact me at:

Unbound Press

Made in the USA
Las Vegas, NV
18 December 2021

38582163R00072